Weird Ireland: A History of Ancient Mysteries, Fantastic Folklore, and Urban Legends Across the Emerald Isle

By Sean McLachlan and Charles River Editors

About Charles River Editors

Charles River Editors provides superior editing and original writing services across the digital publishing industry, with the expertise to create digital content for publishers across a vast range of subject matter. In addition to providing original digital content for third party publishers, we also republish civilization's greatest literary works, bringing them to new generations of readers via ebooks.

Sign up here to receive updates about free books as we publish them, and visit Our Kindle Author Page to browse today's free promotions and our most recently published Kindle titles.

About the Author

Sean McLachlan spent many years working as an archaeologist in Europe, the Middle East, and the United States. Now a full-time writer, he's the author of many history books and novels, including *A Fine Likeness*, a Civil War novel with a touch of the paranormal. Feel free to visit him on his Amazon page and blog.

Introduction

Finlay McWalter's picture of the William Wallace Monument

Weird Ireland

Ireland has a rich folklore. Everyone knows about the fairy folk and leprechauns and many have heard of the fearsome banshee. There are also the usual ghost stories found in every old land. The stranger side of the Emerald Isle goes much deeper than that, however, with tales of phantom armies marching through the sky, sea monsters swimming in the waters around the island, and stories of strange powers and dark magic.

Indeed, these tales are not consigned to the past; many unexplained occurrences continue to happen, even today. Here is a sampling of some of Ireland's odder aspects Ireland. Hopefully, it will inspire readers to learn more about Ireland's mysterious past and unusual present, and perhaps get readers to visit Ireland themselves.

Weird Ireland: A History of Ancient Mysteries, Fantastic Folklore, and Urban Legends Across the Emerald Isle is part of an ongoing series by Sean McLachlan and Charles River Editors that includes *Weird Scotland, Mysterious London,* and more. This book offers a sampling of strange, unexplained, and just plain odd stories from Ireland that have fascinated people in and around the region for centuries. Along with pictures of important people, places, and events, you will learn about Weird Ireland like never before.

Weird Ireland: A History of Ancient Mysteries, Fantastic Folklore, and Urban Legends Across the Emerald Isle

About Charles River Editors

About the Author

Introduction

   An Ancient Mystery

   Strange Creatures of the Deep

   Ghosts, Banshees, and Phantom Ships

   Apparitions of the Blessed Virgin Mary

   Fairy Folk

   Witches, Cunning Folk, and other Magical People

   Watching the Skies

   The Weird and Unexplainable

   Online Resources

   Bibliography

Free Books by Charles River Editors

Discounted Books by Charles River Editors

An Ancient Mystery

Ireland is rich in old stories. The most enduring and global is that of St. Brendan, a 6th century monk who traveled around Britain and Ireland, establishing churches in lands that were still largely Pagan. He also visited remote islands to the west of Ireland, places that became areas of refuge for Irish monks seeking to cut themselves off from the world. Some people believe he even visited North America.

The idea comes from a 9th century manuscript, titled *The Voyage of St. Brendan*. It's a fabulous tale of Brendan and his followers boarding a *currach*—a small, round-bottomed boat made of leather stretched around a wooden frame—and sailing off into the Atlantic on a seven year voyage to find the Promised Land.

After 40 days, they came to an island with steep and rocky cliffs, and waterfalls on the cliffs. There, they discovered a palace filled with food. The devil tempted one of St. Brendan's followers to steal a silver bridle from the palace, but the saint managed to cast the devil out and save the man's soul. Their next stop took them to an island that never experienced winter and had sheep as big as oxen.

Then the real fun began. During the next stage of their trip, they were lifted up by a whale, pestered by demons, chatted with a talking bird, were tossed about by a three-month storm, met Judas Iscariot stranded on a tiny rock in the middle of a stormy sea, and had many other fabulous adventures. The saint, of course, got them through it all with the power of prayer.

A medieval depiction of Brendan and the whale

Here's a typical passage:

> "One day a fish of enormous size appeared swimming after the boat, spouting foam from its nostrils, and ploughing through the waves in rapid pursuit to devour them. Then the brethren cried out to the Lord: 'O Lord, who hast made us, deliver us, Thy servants;' and to St. Brendan they cried aloud: 'Help, O father, help us;' and the saint besought the Lord to deliver His servants, that this monster might not devour them, while he also sought to give courage to the brethren in these words: 'Fear not, you of little faith, for God, who is always our protector, will deliver us from the jaws of this monster, and from every other danger.'
>
> "When the monster was drawing near, waves of immense size rushed on before it,

even up to the gunwale of the boat, which caused the brethren to fear more and more; but St. Brendan, with hands upraised to heaven, earnestly prayed: 'Deliver, O Lord, Thy servants, as Thou didst deliver David from the hands of the giant Goliath, and Jonas from the power of the great whale.'

"When these prayers were uttered, a great monster came into view from the west, and rushing against the other, spouting flame from its mouth, at once attacked it. Then St. Brendan spoke: 'Behold, my children, the wonderful work of our Saviour; see here the obedience of the creature to its Creator: await now the end in safety, for this conflict will bring no evil to us, but only greater glory to God.'

"Thereupon the rueful monster that pursued the servants of God is slain, and cut up in their presence into three parts, and its victor returned whence it came. Next day they saw at a distance an island full of herbage and of wide extent. When they drew near it, and were about to land, they found the hinder portion of the monster that was slain. 'Behold,' said St. Brendan, 'what sought to devour you. Do you now make your food of it, and fill yourselves abundantly with its flesh.'"

Once past these dangers, Brendan and his followers passed through sea choked with ice before coming across a spacious land of thick forest, as much of the northeast coast of North America was at that time. Sailing further, they came to some low, sandy islands that could have been the barrier islands along the Middle Atlantic. Details are sketchy, and for centuries historians have puzzled over the vague geographical hints in an attempt to link them with actual places in the North Atlantic. For example, one island was "remarkably flat, almost level with the sea, without a tree or anything that waved in the wind; but it was of wide extent, and covered over with white and purple flowers." This could be many places in the North Atlantic, from the Orkney Islands just north of Scotland to Arctic Canada. Strangely, this island, and most other places they visited, had already been inhabited by monks.

After a journey of seven years, St. Brendan and his monks finally made it to the Promised Land, and he found it to be a vast country thick with trees and fruit where the sun never sets. Some have tried to link this to northern Canada, where there is almost no night in the summertime. They didn't meet any Native Americans, who were living throughout the region at the time, but they did meet a holy man, or angel, who spoke their language and told them their pilgrimage was over and it was time to go home.

This account, and that of the Vinland Saga of the Norsemen, were both widely known during the Renaissance, and Christopher Columbus himself consulted them before making his historic voyage to the New World. Some medieval maps even drew "St. Brendan's Isle" as being far out in the Atlantic.

A posthumous portrait depicting Columbus

While some modern researchers concede there is much fable in the story, they believe Irish monks could have really sailed across the ocean to the New World. To prove the voyage could have been made, sailor and adventurer Tim Severin built a currach out of traditional materials. The boat measured 36 ft. (11 m), had two masts, and was made of 49 ox hides, lashed together with leather thongs. In 1976, he and his crew sailed it 4,500 miles (7,200 km) from Ireland, across the North Atlantic, to Newfoundland. Everyone made it safely.

It was an epic trip, and Severin's book on the adventure became a bestseller, but while Severin's voyage proves that St. Brendan could have made it across the Atlantic, it doesn't mean that he actually did. After all, unlike St. Brendan, Severin had the advantage of knowing exactly where he was going.

There is, however, evidence that Irish monks got at least part way there. The Faroe Islands, about halfway between Scotland and Iceland, were first settled sometime between the 4th and 6th centuries CE, well before Viking colonization in the 9th century. While material evidence is scant, some scholars believe the settlers were Irish or Scottish monks. Also, in 825, an Irish monk named Dicul wrote that his brethren had colonized islands far to the north of Scotland before the Vikings did.

The Faroes were the first stop in Norse expansion across the North Atlantic. From there, they went on to Iceland, Greenland, and eventually to North America, around 1000.

The first stop was Iceland, which was settled by the Norse around the year 874. Many of the earliest texts from Iceland mention Irish and Scottish monks called *papar*, similar to the Latin and Old Irish words for "Pope." There are also the remains of a settlement at Herjólfsdalur, on the Westman Islands, off Iceland's south coast, that was occupied in the 7th century, well before the Norse said they had made it there. The dating of this site, however, is a matter of dispute in archaeological circles.

The Norseman Erik the Red landed on Greenland in 982, and he returned a few years after to explore and set up two colonies. Though they didn't find any people, they did find the remains of settlements, stone tools, and skin boats. The Norse identified these as belonging to the people of North America they later encountered, but could they have been made by Irish monks, instead? They had already made it halfway across the Atlantic to Iceland. If they had made it to Greenland, they might have discovered there was better land a short sail away in North America, as the Norse had.

Illustration of Erik the Red from Arngrímur Jónsson's *Gronlandia*

The evidence for this, however, is lacking. There is no archaeological evidence supporting the presence of Irish colonies in North America. No settlements – such as the famous Skellig Michael (recently featured in *Star Wars: The Force Awakens*) – have survived and no distinctly Irish medieval artifacts have been found. Thus, unless archaeologists dig up any solid proof from the ground, the Legend of St. Brendan will have to stay a legend. Irish-Americans can at least be comforted by the fact that he could have made it, and even if he didn't, his name will always be associated with the exploration of the New World.

Strange Creatures of the Deep

While their Scottish neighbors to the east can boast having the most well-known lake monsters–the most famous, of course, at Loch Ness–the Irish can also claim to have a few beasties living in their lakes as well.

The most famous is Muckie, said to dwell in the Lakes of Killarney, a series of three lovely lakes in County Kerry. In recent years, several people claim to have sighted a large grey object with two or more humps rising above the surface before quickly disappearing into the depths. In 2003, when a team of marine biologists did a sonar scan of the lakes to detect the fish population, they noted a large object in the water that they couldn't identify.

Muckross Lake, one of the Lakes of Killarney

A picture of the lakes from Torc Mountain

Then there are the fearsome Dobhar-chú, said to lurk in many Irish rivers. Unlike the reclusive, benign Muckie, the Dobhar-chú are not to be trifled with. Having haunted Irish rivers since ancient times, they often surface in pairs or groups to drag unlucky people into the water. They are said to look like giant otters or a mix between a dog and a fish. Dobhar-chú means "water hound" in Old Irish. In modern Irish, it means "otter," further obscuring the real nature of this beast.

Whatever they are, they still capture the imagination of the rural Irish, who have no doubt of the creatures' existence. Their fierceness is attested on a 17th century gravestone, called the Kinlough Stone, dedicated to the memory of a woman named Gráinne, who was attacked by the Dobhar-chú as she was washing the family's clothes by the shore of Glenade Lough. Her screams attracted her husband, who killed the beast, but not before his wife had succumbed. As the Dobhar-chú fell, it let out a whistling sound summoning another Dobhar-chú, probably its mate. The farmer managed to kill that one as well.

A Bango Art depiction of a Dobhar-chú

While rare, sightings of the Dobhar-chú still occur today. Irish artist Sean Corcoran and his wife described the creature as covered with gray fur except for its orange webbed feet in 2003.

The seas around the Emerald Isle are thick with monsters. Perhaps the most famous of these has been sighted for many years off the coast of Kilkee, County Clare. Kilkee became a popular beach resort in Victorian times, and visitors who flocked to the little village on Ireland's west coast to stroll along the picturesque shore got to see more than they'd expected.

The Kilkee cliffs

In 1850, numerous witnesses spotted a large sea serpent sunning itself near the shore. It was said to have resembled many other sea monsters spotted in the 19th century—a long, serpentine beast with a large head and smooth gray or black skin. The creature was seen numerous times, making headlines in September of 1871, when several witnesses recounted their sightings for the press. Europe's popular illustrated newspapers, filled with engravings of current events, showed a long, snakelike creature with flippers and huge eyes, threatening a group of ladies on shore with its fanged maw. A gentleman is shown bravely defending the "weaker sex" as they flee in horror, but more it's more than likely the man was running as well.

A report in the October 1871 edition of *Daily Doings* said of the monster, "It had an enormous head, shaped somewhat like a horse, while behind the head and on the neck was a huge mane of seaweed-looking water; the eyes were large and glaring, and, by the appearance of the water behind, a vast body seemed to be beneath the waves."

Sightings of sea serpents were fairly common in the age of steam, but sadly, there are fewer sea monsters to contend with now. Some people will scoff and say that modern people are less likely to believe in such nonsense, while others point out that the pollution of our oceans might have made them go extinct, or at least put them on the endangered list.

They haven't disappeared completely, however. In 2013, some fishermen in Lough Foyle, which opens onto the North Channel, caught a weird sea creature on film. The minute of footage shows a dark gray or black hump moving smoothly through the water. The hump was peaked at the top and had several irregular bumps on its surface. It sped along at about the speed of a man jogging, neither rising nor falling for several seconds before gradually descending into the water and out of sight. It left little wake and seemed to be headed out to sea. The film shows it passing between the photographer's boat and another boat, thus allowing for an estimate of the hump's size. It appears to rise about a meter above the water and to be two or so meters long. Of course, this is only the part that was visible above the water. Its actual dimensions could be much greater.

Ghosts, Banshees, and Phantom Ships

For those who believe in them, an ancient land like Ireland is bound to be thickly populated by ghosts. Irish folklore is rich in ghost stories, and many sightings and strange experiences continue to the present day.

One lovely tradition from the 19th and 20th centuries says that the spirits of migrants who have died overseas would return home as seagulls or sea mist. But not all Irish ghost stories are as poetic; in fact, some are downright ghoulish. For example, the little town of Rathkeale, County Limerick, stands Holy Trinity Church and its historic cemetery. While the present church is relatively recent, having been built in 1831, there has been a church in that location for more than 700 years, and the cemetery has graves dating back more than 300 years. For many years, the graveyard is said to have been haunted by a female specter so frightening to look upon that those who see her have their hearts stop.

One local man, braver than most, stayed in the graveyard overnight armed with his trusty sword, waiting for the ghost. Why he thought he'd be able to kill a ghost with a sword is anyone's guess, but he had great faith in God and the Virgin Mary, and for an Irishman, that was good enough. The ghost duly appeared and the man looked at it full in the face, fearing nothing.

He took one swipe at it with his sword, cut off the ghost's arm, and the phantom woman vanished out of sight. The man spent the rest of the night praying the woman's restless spirit would be laid to rest, and it never appeared again.

Oddly, another supernatural woman made her appearance in a graveyard in the same small town, but this time, the experience was far more benign (as discussed further below in the section on Marian apparitions).

As is the case in other old countries, many historic buildings are said to be haunted. One of these haunted buildings is Ross Castle, on the shores of Lough Sheelin, County Meath, which has earned the dubious distinction of being considered the most haunted castle in Ireland. The region had a bloody history in the Middle Ages, having been just "beyond the pale," meaning it was past the area of English control. With the English to the east and the native Celtic tribes to the west and north, the area became a constant battleground. Several castles and strongholds dotted the landscape at the time. Ross Castle was built in 1533 by the English to control the River Inny where it enters Lough Sheelin. This was the outer limits of their territory, and thus the castle was of crucial strategic importance. It suffered many sieges and battles before it was eventually leveled by Oliver Cromwell after it had been used as a base for Irish rebels.

A 19th century picture of Ross Castle

A modern picture of Ross Castle

Cromwell

Naturally, such a place was ripe for haunting. Most of the stories center around Richard Nugent, the 12th Lord of Delvin, the man who built the castle in 1536. He was a tough and cruel man, even by the standards of those tough and cruel times, and it eventually earned him the nickname of the Black Baron. Some locals say this was due to his having hanged an innocent beggar whom he accused of stealing some bread, even though there had been no evidence against the man.

Blood does not always run true, and the Black Baron's daughter was said to be as kind as he was cruel; as sweet as he was bitter. Her name was Sabina, and everyone loved her. She could often be seen strolling on the shores of the Lough Sheelin, where she would admire the view and speak with anyone she met without prejudice. Even though she was the daughter of an English military occupier, she chatted happily with the Irish peasants she met. This made her as well loved by the Irish as she was by the English.

Given her position, she was supposed to be accompanied by a chaperone at all times. Sabina had a free spirit, however, and often slipped away to walk alone, knowing she had nothing to fear.

It was on one of those solitary walks that she met a handsome young man and started talking with him. His name was Orwin O'Reilly, the son of a local Irish chief. They formed an instant attraction for one another and promised to meet again, soon. Neither Sabina nor Orwin were so young and innocent as to be unaware of the dangers of their friendship. Their fathers were enemies, after all, as were their respective peoples, and they had to have their meetings in the utmost of secrecy. As the meetings continued, their love grew, as did their despair. They wanted to get married, but this was impossible; simply meeting together as they did was bound to cause a war.

Like other star-crossed lovers throughout time, they decided to elope. One night, Sabina slipped out of Ross Castle and crept to the shore of Lough Sheelin, where Orwin waited for her with a boat. They rowed out across the water, their young hearts filled with hope for the future that they would settle down somewhere far away from their warring fathers and start a new life under new names.

As the lovers talked of the future, a sudden storm blew in from the west. Orwin tried to manage the oars while Sabina bailed desperately, but it was no use. The storm grew stronger, eventually overturning the boat and sending the couple into the frigid waters of Lough Sheelin. Sabina was found the next morning, washed up on shore and barely alive. She was carried back to Ross Castle where she lay unconscious for three days. When she, at last, awoke, it was to terrible news - her lover, Orwin, had been found as well, but he had drowned. Sabina fell into despair and locked herself in the tower, refusing to eat or drink until she, too, had died. Perhaps she hoped to join her lover on the other side, but it was not to be. Instead, she haunts the castle, endlessly roaming its halls or looking over its battlements with the hope of finding her long-lost lover, her sorrowful wailing awakening residents.

A picture of Lough Sheelin

The Black Baron is sometimes seen, too. According to local legend, Sabina's stay on this earth will only end when her evil father has atoned for his misdeeds.

Ross Castle is now a bed and breakfast, and online guest reviews tell of the many strange occurrences happening there. Besides seeing both ghosts, one visitor was scratched on the arm by invisible nails, cutting so deeply they drew blood. Others hear strains of old music, feel sudden drops in temperature, and are awoken by phantom footsteps in the hall. The hauntings center around the tower, the oldest part of the castle, although entities have been seen, heard, and felt all over the newer portions built in the last two centuries, as well. Of all the rooms in the bed and breakfast, the most haunted is the Whisper Room, so called because guests there often hear whispering that seems to come from thin air.

Even for those who don't believe in ghosts, a stay in an old castle is a memorable experience. Ross Castle is decorated with suits of armor, stuffed birds, and even a buffalo's head, which–while not exactly Irish–certainly adds an odd atmosphere to the place. Several other Irish castles have been turned into similar B&Bs as well, such as Clontarf Castle in Dublin, Ashford Castle in County Mayo, Ballynahinch Castle in County Connemara, and many more. All of them, it seems, have a ghost story to tell.

Many of Ireland's traditional pubs are believed to be haunted as well. John Kavanagh's in Dublin, locally known as "The Gravediggers Pub," dates back to 1833, making it a relative youngster when compared to the city's historic buildings. It gets its nickname thanks to being located next to the historic Glasnevin Cemetery, where many prominent Irish figures, such as Irish nationalists Stewart Parnell and Roger Casement, are buried. The pub was where the gravediggers were known to refresh themselves after a hard day's work, often making their orders by throwing a clod of dirt against the wall in order to alert the barkeep. At night, it was said to be the den of grave robbers. It is still a solemn place, with no singing or dancing allowed, and no television that ruins the atmosphere of so many old pubs. There isn't even a telephone.

Parnell

Casement

On some quiet nights, a visitor might notice an old man in an out of date tweed suit, sipping a pint at the end of the bar. He doesn't speak, and is so unremarkable that no one bothers to speak to him, but when he finishes his drink he simply fades away.

The most famous Irish ghost is, of course, the banshee, a female spirit that lets out a loud wail at night. There are two traditions that explain their existence. One is that she is the ghost of a woman who lost her children before she died. This tradition can be found in other cultures as well, such as the Mexican belief in *La Llorona* ("The Weeping Woman"). The other explanation for the banshee is that of a fairy, come to mourn humans who have died–often but not necessarily children–or to warn a family that they would soon suffer a loss. The term banshee comes from the Irish *bean sidhe*, meaning "woman of the fairies." The banshee was attached to certain families, always of the aristocratic class, who would hear her mournful keening before one of their number was about to die.

In Shane's Castle on the shores of Lough Neah in Antrim, there's a room reserved for a banshee. She is said to appear regularly, sometimes hooded and hard to see, sometimes looking like a beautiful but mournful young maiden. Family tradition states that the banshee is actually the spirit of a member of the castle's hereditary family, the O'Neills. It was a girl named Kathleen, who was taken away by the fairy folk, only allowed to return when a member of the family was about to die.

Kenneth Allen's picture of the ruins of Shane's Castle

Another female spirit is the fearsome Demon Bride. This baleful ghost has haunted the Errigal-Truagh Graveyard in County Monaghan for more than two centuries. It waits until there is a funeral in the graveyard, watching the mourners carefully. As the grieving family and friends file out of the cemetery, one person will often linger for a moment. If this final mourner is a young man, the Demon Bride appears as a beautiful young woman and chats with the fellow, whose sadness turns to interest at the attentions of the comely stranger. The Demon Bride tells the young man how handsome he is and how much she fancies him. At this point, she gets him to promise to return to the cemetery exactly one month later, in order to get "better acquainted." They seal the promise with a kiss, a kiss so passionate that the man is fired with lust.

At that point the lady vanishes. The young man blinks in surprise, not sure what has happened. As he staggers out of the graveyard, he remembers the local tale of the Demon Bride, and realizes he's lost his soul to a spirit from the other side, which makes him go mad, his raving terror destroying his health until he dies. Exactly one month after he's met the Demon Bride, he keeps his promise by being buried in the Errigal-Truagh Graveyard.

Besides dead individuals stalking the land and Ireland's old buildings, there are also phantom ships that roam the seas in the area. Several of them are known from the vicinity of Wexford, where they seem to gather.

One morning in 1915, a tugboat left Wexford Harbour, heading for the Tuskar Rock lighthouse off Ireland's southeast coast. World War I was in the process of ripping Europe apart, and the crew had been told to keep a sharp eye out for warships and U-boats. As the boat got out into the open ocean, the crew spotted a warship in the distance, headed in their direction. As was normal for the time, the crew raised the Union Jack to identify themselves. Ireland had not yet achieved its independence, and the Union Jack was the flag the Irish crew flew, whether they liked it or not. Hoping the warship wasn't German, they watched with bated breath to see which flag the ship would send up. But the ship didn't put up a flag. It passed close by the tugboat, and while the crew was able to see the men on board, they could not read the name of the ship on the prow, nor could they see any signs to identify the ship's country of origin.

When the tugboat arrived at the Tuskar Rock lighthouse, they told the lighthouse keeper what they had seen, and were shocked to learn that the keeper hadn't seen any warships pass by at all that day. The lighthouse keeper had a splendid view of the entire area and would certainly have spotted any vessel as it passed, especially if it were a warship in a time of national emergency. The warship was never seen again, and no one ever discovered which side it belonged to, or if it even existed at all.

A very different kind of tugboat lurks around the Saltee Islands, two small islands three miles off the coast of County Wexford. Sometimes, an unidentified tugboat is seen steaming around the islands, and once darkness falls, strange lights are seen just offshore. When fishermen see this, they stay at home mending their nets and salting the day's catch, because they know these are signs of a bad storm brewing and that it would be suicide to go out on that night.

Another ghost ship is regularly seen off the shore of the Great Saltee, the bigger of the two islands. Around the turn of the last century, two men went out onto the rough seas with a rowboat to see if they could save the crew of a shipwreck off the island's south coast–they never returned. The rowboat sometimes returns to the dock on moonless nights. Though it's always dark when it appears, the boat can be clearly made out, and you can hear the oars as they are pulled from their oarlocks and stowed away.

Apparitions of the Blessed Virgin Mary

Ireland is a deeply religious country. Most people are Catholic, and the Church is a cornerstone of social life. Because of this, it is not surprising there have been several accounts of religious miracles, especially sightings of the Virgin Mary, many of which have occurred in the modern day and have supposedly been caught on camera.

Perhaps the most famous in modern times is the rocking statue of the Virgin Mary at Ballinspittle grotto, a roadside grotto featuring a life-sized plaster statue of Mary on a low hill. On July 22, 1985, Cathy O'Mahony and her mother, who lived near the grotto, stopped by to visit. The grotto has a few benches where the devout can sit and pray while looking up at the statue. As they sat down to pray, they noticed the statue had begun to rock back and forth. Convinced they had seen a miracle, they brought more people to the grotto the next day, and they, too, saw the statue rock.

The grotto

Soon, the little roadside shrine was besieged with thousands of people from across the country. The sightings made international news. In all, an estimated 100,000 people visited the previously little-known shrine that summer. On August 15, the Feast of Assumption, an estimated 20,000 people flooded the area, during which some people claimed to have seen the statue floating in the air. One man told reporters he had seen the face of Jesus superimposed on the statue.

The Catholic Church remained neutral on the subject. Michael Murphy, the Bishop of Cork and Ross, issued a public statement that the worshippers had fallen prey to an optical illusion. He went on to say that "direct supernatural intervention is a very rare happening in life. So, common sense would demand that we approach the claims made concerning the grotto at Ballinspittle with prudence and caution. Before a definite pronouncement could be made by the Church, all natural explanations would have to be examined and exhausted over a lengthy period of time."

Regardless, the events in the Ballinspittle grotto set off a wave of religious sightings across the country. In some 30 locations, other statues of Mary – or various saints – moved, and religious figures appeared on church walls.

Ballinspittle grotto, however, remained the focus of attention, and not all of it good. A group of Pentecostals showed up one day, screamed about idolatry, and smashed the statue with hammers. It was soon repaired and went back to rocking and attracting pilgrims.

On the 30th anniversary of the start of the sightings, the *Irish Examiner* reported that the roadside grotto remained a pilgrimage site. Cathy O'Mahony still insists that what she saw was real, as do several other locals.

In an even stranger story, the July 8, 2009 issue of *The Telegraph* reported that workers cutting down a tree in the cemetery of Holy Mary Parish Church in Rathkeale, County Limerick noticed the stump was shaped like a hooded figure holding a smaller figure. One of the workmen immediately fell to his knees and crossed himself, sure he was seeing an apparition of the Blessed Virgin Mary. Word spread fast in the small town, which has a population of only 1,500, and before long people flocked to see the stump, coming in from other towns and counties. A candlelight vigil attracted an estimated 700 people. Others were more skeptical, including a local priest who said it was "just a tree." The Catholic Church avoids taking positions in such cases for fear the religion will fall into superstition, but it doesn't stop the vigils or pilgrimages from other parishes. The Church says that people getting together to pray is always a good thing.

If that wasn't strange enough, the Virgin Mary appeared again seven years later, this time on the side of a house about 20 miles down the road in Kilmallock. One night in December 2016, someone noticed something unusual on the side of a house on the Riverview Estate—a glistening, sparkling shape that looked like a hooded figure holding a smaller figure. As was the case with the tree stump, this was taken to be the Blessed Virgin Mary with the Baby Jesus. A crowd soon gathered despite the chill, and photos of the shape went viral on the Internet. The shape disappeared the next day, and while many dismissed it as a shape caused by frost, others insisted their housing estate had been treated to a genuine sighting of the Mother of God.

The Irish are generally divided on these apparitions. Many devout Catholics think people are deluding themselves when they think they see a statue floating in the air or the shape of the Virgin Mary in a tree stump. As Bishop Murphy said, the Church feels such miracles are rare. Even the Bible, which is full of miracles, treats them as something special and unusual. Despite these objections, there are many in Ireland who truly believe in these miracles, as it helps them in their faith and in facing life's many challenges. Psychologists and anthropologists point out that waves of religious miracles tend to occur in difficult years. The 1980s saw bad economic times in Ireland, and the Emerald Isle is currently going through another economic recession and experiencing another wave of miracles. Social scientists say that the sightings are a way for people to deal with their troubles. True believers, on the other hand, point out that God makes Himself known at the very times needed to keep people's faith strong.

Fairy Folk

No discussion of Ireland's paranormal traditions would be complete without talking about the fairy folk, or the "wee folk," as the Irish sometimes call them. The Irish use other names, too: the Good People; the Little People; the Noble People; the People of the Hills; and most eloquently, the People Outside Us. In the Irish language, they were also called the *Sidhe* or the *Feadh-Ree*, the origin of the term "fairy."

Fairies were supposed to be fallen angels from when Lucifer rebelled against God. As God was casting them out, St. Michael interceded, asking the Creator not to cast any more out lest Heaven would be empty. God agreed, declaring the angels should remain where they were at that moment. Some had already fallen to Hell, while others were still in Heaven. Others had fallen from Heaven and made it halfway to Hell, thus residing on Earth, and those ones became the fairies.

In traditional Irish culture, fairies weren't considered remote creatures on the edge of reality. Rather, they lived right alongside human beings, and evidence of their existence could be seen everywhere. Prehistoric burial mounds were thought to be their homes– sometimes called a *lios* ("fairy fort"). Ancient flint arrowheads were said to be made by fairies.

Fairies are not necessarily dangerous - in fact, they can be quite helpful – but they are easily offended and must be handled with care. When building a house, people must take care not to build it on one of the fairies' homes or to block one of the fairies' paths. Since the roads of the wee folk are difficult to spot, it's best to test the site. Before building a house, set sticks down where corners of the foundation are to go, and if the sticks are still in place the next day, then everything will be fine. If, however, the sticks have been moved, it is a sign that the fairy folk don't want any construction at that spot, and it's best to find another location.

At the same time, it's unwise to move the location too far away, because having fairies on the property ensures a good harvest and that the flocks and herds will prosper. Fairies shared in the wealth of the farm, as long as the farmer was smart and offered them some of his bounty. In some locations, a bowl of milk or butter was left out for them, a practice that is seen in many places in Europe, and as far away as Denmark. Cows that have just given birth to a calf were held in special esteem, and the first stream of milk from such a cow was shot onto the ground so the fairies could lap it up.

Sharing with the fairies helped get people on their good side, but it was best to be cautious.

Red ribbons were tied to the cows' tails or necks to protect them, and on St. Brigid's Eve, an important festival, crosses made of straw are hung in the byre. St. Brigid's Feast, which falls on February 1, marks the start of agricultural work and was an important festival, even in pre-Christian times. Many strange customs were associated with the feast. For example, on Ireland's coast, fishermen brought shellfish into their homes and placed them in the four corners, in order to ensure a good catch for the rest of the year.

If a child spilled milk on the ground, the parents would state, "That to the fairies, leave it to them and welcome." The child wouldn't be scolded, lest it appear as if the parents begrudged the fairies their due. Similarly, when throwing dirty water out of the house, people called out, "Mind the water." In doing so, they hoped to avoid splashing fairies who may be lurking nearby. Fairies are an arrogant lot, and to ruin their fine clothing with a splash of water would surely invoke their wrath.

In the days when many a farmer was known to supplement his income with the profits from an illegal whisky still, the first drops of any batch were thrown up toward the roof as an offering to Red Willie, a fairy who looked over whisky production and who probably got his name from the florid features he developed as a result of too much drinking. If Red Willie received his offering, he'd be sure to protect the still from the police and the taxman.

If one angered the wee folk, one might find his cow "elf shot," evidenced by a small cut in the skin and the presence of a flint arrowhead nearby. The cow would languish, stop producing milk, and perhaps even die. With so many farmers living on the edge of poverty, the loss of a single cow could be a disaster, so the cunning folk developed many cures for elf-shot cows, one of which was to place a fairy arrow in some water, boil the water, and get the cow to drink it.

Fairies lived much like humans, with homes, farms, families, and livestock. They even had wars. Sometimes, a farmer would set out across his field in the early morning, and in addition to the usual dew, he would see a strange white liquid spread over the grass. This was said to be fairy blood, spilt during a fierce battle the night before.

Just like humans, fairies liked the good things in life. All of their men were handsome, and all their women beautiful. They drank nectar out of flowers and the table settings for their feasts were made of pure gold. Despite their wealth, the fairies coveted fine cattle and beautiful babies, and weren't above stealing them. This was the origin of the infamous "changeling." Sometimes, a mother would put her lovely newborn to bed, only to wake up the next morning to find a sickly, wizened, squalling brat in the crib the next morning. This changeling was said to be a baby rejected from the fairy world. Assuming it survived childhood, it would end up being an evil adult who would cause trouble throughout the district. Cattle could be switched out with changelings as well.

Unbaptized children were in the most danger of being taken. Of course, any good Catholic parent would try to carry out this ritual as soon as possible, but in the more remote areas of the countryside, there might be a long wait. Thus, to keep the fairies at bay, it was a good idea to sew some salt into the baby's clothing.

Children could even be switched while still in the womb. A sure sign the fairies were attempting to do this was that the pregnant woman would suddenly turn sickly. If this happened, one was to open every press and drawer in the house in order to ease childbirth. Once the child was born, they had to be closed immediately up again to trap the fairies inside so they wouldn't be able to take the baby. The fairies had to be kept there until a red coal was placed under the cradle and a branch tied over it—alder for a boy or mountain ash for a girl. Then, the salt had to be sewn into the child's clothing before the occupants of the house could finally open their drawers again.

Some cunning men and women knew the secret to seeing the usually invisible fairies. They developed an ointment–the recipe for which was a closely guarded secret–that when rubbed into the eyes, allowed the user see the invisible world. One had to take care, however, because as everyone knows, the fairies like their privacy. If they ever noticed a human who was able to see them, they'd pop the person's eyes out.

While much of Irish lore deals with placating the wee folk, there are times when fairies actually help humans. Sometimes, a poor farmer will be behind on his rent or taxes and be harassed by the debt collector. When the debt collector heads for the poor family's farm, ready to turn them out for lack of payment, he might meet a stranger on the road who will tell him he intends to pay the family's debt, giving him the exact sum owed. Once the payment has been marked in the ledger, the debt collector returns home, only to discover the coins have turned into leaves in his pocket.

Though the Irish believed in and respected fairies in the olden days, they never worshipped them. Fairies were inferior creatures, lacking an immortal soul, and the Irish believed they would be wiped out forever come the Day of Judgment. Only human beings had a chance at an eternal life in heaven.

Witches, Cunning Folk, and other Magical People

As is the case in all traditional societies, Ireland had its share of people who didn't quite fit in. Some were considered forces of good, while others committed nothing but evil.

Irish witches often appeared as simple farmers or fishermen who happened to have aknowledge of magic. They often sucked the luck out of neighboring farms in order to prosper while others suffered. May Eve and May Day were dangerous times, when people were said to be at the mercy of these witches, as well as fairy folk. It was said the fairy forts lay open at that time and the fairies moved freely about the land. It was at this time that fairies often moved houses, and it was an unwise traveler who ventured out late at night.

Taking advantage of this magical festival, witches would try to steal luck from their neighbors. One way to do this was to remove several bucketfuls of water from a neighbor's well, splashing toward their own house. Throwing salt and holy water into a well would protect people from this. Another method was to draw a rope along the dew of a neighbor's field on May Morn, whispering, "Come all to me." This would bring all the production of milk and butter to the witch's house.

One trick the witches had was to turn themselves into hares and drink milk from the cows at night. The best way to get rid of these magical hares was to shoot them with a silver bullet made from an old florin coin. The florin, a silver coin with a cross stamped on, proved doubly effective against witches, due to the combination of the silver and the cross.

Witches had various secrets and tools of the trade, but none was more powerful than the Dead Man's Hand. This was exactly as it sounds—the hand of a recently departed man, stolen from the graveyard at the stroke of midnight. It was dried and smoked until it had the consistency of leather. The Dead Man's Hand could then be used to cast spells and enact curses. Some of these hands were passed down through generations of witches and have ended up in modern collections.

On the more benign side of the magical arts, there were cunning folk who could be relied upon to perform cures and cast spells to bring good luck and drive away the bad. Some people received this status due to a family tradition of handing it down from generation to generation. Others got it by being born under special circumstances, such as being the seventh son of the seventh son, or having been born after one's father had died.

One group of cunning folk was known to have healed the sick with various herbal remedies. Modern medical science is only just scratching the surface of this old knowledge and has so far found that many traditional cures have at least a partial basis in reality. Other cures, however, don't help at all. Even though the herbalists had some level of success, they were considered to be the lowest level of cunning folk. Ireland's traditional folk preferred magical cures. In fact, the more outlandish the remedy, the more it was in favor.

Take, for example, the cure for ague. This antiquated term referred to any disease causing fever and shivering. To cure someone suffering from ague, the cunning man or woman would wrap a living spider in a cobweb. This was then put into a lump of butter and eaten while the patient was in the midst of a shivering fit.

This disgusting concoction pales in comparison to the cure for epilepsy, which involved taking nine pieces of a dead man's skull, grinding them into powder, and mixing it with a fern called wall rue. The epileptic is supposed to take a spoonful of the stuff on an empty stomach every morning for nine days until he is cured (or begins to hide his ailment in order to avoid taking any more of the medicine). He'd better finish it all, however, because if any was left over, the dead man was bound to return, looking for the missing bits of his skull.

Those suffering from persistent headaches could avoid these horrible cures by going to the most specialized of healers: the measuring doctor. The measuring doctor only worked on certain days, according to some complex numerological formula. If the patient visited on the right day, the measuring doctor would sit the sufferer down and measure the man's head. Measurements were taken from ear to ear across the forehead, from ear to ear over the crown of the head, and diagonally across the head. The diagnosis would always be the same: the patient's head was "too open." To cure this, the measuring doctor would press on the head while whispering certain prayers. The patient would have to return for three days in a row, and each time the measuring doctor would measure and press, measure and press, until finally declaring that the patient's skull had finally closed. Proof of his efficacy was that the measurements he took became smaller each day, until the final diagnosis of a closed skull had taken all of the sufferer's pain away.

For those who didn't trust the cunning folk or who weren't fortunate enough to have one living nearby, there were various cures one could try on oneself. For example, if you suffered from bad vision or sore eyes, a visit to a holy well would help. There were holy wells all over Ireland, many of them attached to old ruins, some of them with Pagan origins. Some of the more powerful holy wells were said to have been able to cure blindness.

Holy wells had to be treated with the proper rituals and reverence. They must be approached with a respectful demeanor, and circumambulated three or nine times, depending on the well. Some wells required you to walk around them, while others required you to go on your hands and knees, but in all cases, it was from east to west, following the path of the sun, a hint at the Pagan origins of the wells. While doing this, the pilgrim must recite Pater Nosters and Ave Marias. After each circuit, the faithful must add a stone to a pile nearby, to be counted by the angels at the time of the Last Judgment. Those with the most stones will go on to the highest level of Heaven. Once this ritual has been completed, the person may approach the well itself, which was usually down a flight of narrow steps to an underground pool. They had to then bathe their face and hands in the well to get the effect of that particular well, or drink the water, if that was what was required. Some wells were known to have cured a whole range of diseases, while others treated eye trouble, arthritis, or other common ailments.

Many wells date to Pagan times, and have standing stones nearby or are shaded by an ash tree, which was a tree sacred to Celtic druids. With these wells, it is customary to give some offering to the tree or stones, usually in the form of a colorful ribbon tied around them. While in ancient times these were offerings to the local spirit, god, or goddess, in Christian times they were, and are, offerings to the patron saint of the well. These offerings should not be removed or the magic will be lost, thus they remain throughout the year, fading and tattering in the wind until nature makes them fall off by themselves.

Holy wells weren't the only places to go to look for a cure. Those with a toothache need only go to a graveyard, kneel down at a grave, say three Pater Nosters, three Ave Marias, and then grab a handful of grass growing on top of the grave. This was to be chewed without swallowed, and bits of it pulled from the mouth and tossed away until it was all gone. It was said that the brave soul who did this would never suffer from a toothache again for as long as he lived.

Some illnesses were caused by the fairies and couldn't be cured by simple remedies. These were called "fairy strokes" and were considered very serious. In these cases, a very effective cure dating far back into Ireland's past was in order. Three rows of salt of equal length had to be placed on a table. The afflicted would then have their arm put around the rows enclosing them, have their head bent over the salt, and the Lord's Prayer would be said three times over each row. Next, take the hand of the patient, who is usually too far gone to perform the spell themselves, and recite, "By the power of the Father, and of the Son, and of the Holy Spirit, let this disease depart, and the spell of the evil spirits be broken! I adjure, I command you, to leave this man/woman (insert name here). In the name of God I pray; in the name of Christ I adjure; in the name of the Spirit of God I command and compel you to go back and leave this man free! AMEN! AMEN! AMEN!"

If the victim of the fairy stroke was a child, there was a different cure. First, all the windows and doors of the house had to be securely shut in order to keep the fairies from seeing what was going on, or they might come in and disrupt the cure. A big fire had to be built, into which a packet of herbs, prepared by one of the cunning folk, was thrown. The child had to be carried around the fire three times, while reciting certain secret phrases provided by the cunning folk and sprinkling holy water into the flame. If the child sneezed three times - a likely occurrence given that the house would be filled with smoke by then – he or she was cured and the curse of the fairies was lifted, never to be put on again. To be on the safe side, however, it was best to tie a small bag around the child's neck containing three red ribbons, the nail from the shoe of an ass, and some hair from a black cat. This needed to be worn for a year and a day.

Similar to the cunning folk were certain priests who were considered to have magical powers to heal and protect. Oddly enough, young priests who had just taken the cloth were considered to be more magical than their older superiors. Also, "silenced priests," those who had been suspended for some infraction, were considered the most powerful of all. Why this is the case isn't quite clear. Perhaps it was the common thread of rebellion found in many Catholic countries, where the Church was revered and mistrusted in equal measure.

These magical priests were relied upon to heal the sick, stop the plans of evil landlords, and bring good luck. Sometimes, they didn't even need to be asked to perform these services. If you could get an article of their clothing or even some dirt from their graves, it might be enough.

Watching the Skies

While Ireland isn't famous for its UFOs - that distinction goes to the United States - the Irish have been seeing them in their skies long before it was trendy to do so.

A global wave of UFO sightings occurred in 1947 after businessman Kenneth Arnold flew a private plane over Mt. Rainier in Washington and reported seeing nine "peculiar looking aircraft" flying in a V formation. He said they were shaped like discs and "flew like a saucer would if you skipped it across the water." The story made international headlines, and the term "flying saucer" was born.

While the wave of UFO sightings in the late '40s and early '50s is often remembered as the first wave of UFO sightings, it was actually the second. The first started a half century earlier in 1896, when mysterious airships were spotted all across North America. While crude airships or dirigibles already existed at the time, the airships people reported seeing were much larger and faster, and they appeared in great numbers across Canada and the United States for a span of 20 years.

They came over to Ireland, too, although they took their time. The first airship sighting occurred in 1909, when, on May 19 of that year, an oblong shape was spotted by residents of Belfast flying over the sea, lit up with a string of brilliant lights.

There was another sighting the next day. On May 21, the *Irish Times* reported that the evening before, a mysterious airship had been seen over Donnybrook by numerous witnesses. One described it as a "large oblong shell," while others said it was shaped like a sphere. It moved over the town at a high altitude at considerable speed, even though the night was still, leading people to conclude it must have been powered instead of being a simple balloon. Earlier that afternoon, a similar airship "illuminated by two strong lights" had been seen on the outskirts of Kingstown (now known as Dún Laoghaire), a few miles to the southeast. The airship was seen to have moved to the southwest, and the Donnybrook sightings told of the craft coming from the west and passing over the town in an easterly direction. Could this have been the same airship having made a loop inland before scaring the good residents of Donnybrook?

It wouldn't be the last time. The next year, some fishermen just off the coast of Doagh, County Donegal got a bad fright. On the evening of May 6, a group of fishermen looked up from their work to watch what they had first thought to be a large steamer on the horizon. It soon became apparent that this was no steamer when the bluish-gray object headed right for the shore a quarter of a mile from them. Thinking it was about to smash on the rocks, they sailed over to it in order to help any survivors.

When they got there, they saw the ship was hovering over the beach, "with a dipping motion, at an average of about 20 feet above sea level." The fishermen described it as "being in the form of a torpedo boat, but larger and broader, and carrying with it a steam-like vapor which prevented detection of its exact shape." Torpedo boats were light, narrow ships built for speed, and as the flying torpedo boat - or whatever it was - passed over the beach, there was a large explosion. Later, when three beached fishing boats were found to have been damaged, the fishermen blamed the mystery airship. It continued inland, passing over a field where it set off another explosion. Steam rose from the field below, and a cow was badly cut up.

At this point, it appeared as if the strange apparition was bombing Ireland. The ship then passed over the town of Legacurry, some twenty miles to the south, and "the residents of the village, hearing deafening noise overhead, rushed out of their houses in a state of consternation. It is stated that the noise did not resemble thunder so nearly as it did the roar of a huge waterfall." Then came "a dull thud, as if of a falling substance." Residents later discovered that a mud bank near the town "had been furrowed as if with a gigantic plough for over twenty yards." It continued to the town of Malin, where it made "a tremendous sound like that of a violent hail storm" before passing out of sight.

The coastguard opined that it could have been one of several dirigibles recently lost at sea, although why a distressed crew would bomb people on the ground rather than signal for help could not be explained. The locals weren't having any of that story, either, and according to the May 14, 1910 edition of the *Dundalk Examiner*, they "[spoke] of the visitation as being of quite an unearthly description, and pray[ed] they may be spared a recurrence of it."

So what were these strange airships? They appeared to be faster and more numerous than the airships that actually existed in their day and their actions were strange. Some UFO researchers theorized that UFO sightings have changed through the years in keeping with the culture of the time. People see a strange object in the sky and try to rationalize it based on what they know. Thus, ancient people saw flying gods or angels, and people in the 19th century and early 20th century saw airships. By the time Kenneth Arnold had made his famous sighting, science fiction was all the rage, so people were prepared to see such strange spaceships. Whether UFOs are, in fact, visitors from outer space remains hotly debated in UFO circles. While it is the majority opinion among Ufologists, others believe the craft to be visitors from another time or dimension, or may even be living creatures.

There have been a host of UFO sightings in modern Ireland. Two spectacular cases will suffice to stand in for the rest. In June 1997, an Aer Lingus flight was heading from Dublin to London when the pilot and copilot noticed a glowing red object with blue and white stripes heading straight for them. They were so startled that they took evasive action. The UFO soon disappeared, and when the pilots reported the incident, air traffic control found no radar record showing another airplane near them at the time.

In another case on May 1, 2011, four witnesses in Arklow, County Wicklow, saw a brilliant white light over the River Avoca. The object appeared to be round in shape and shimmered, changing to other colors. It appeared to be 1,000-2,000 feet above the ground and moved at incredible speed and occasionally stopping abruptly, something that aircraft and meteors cannot do. The witnesses watched it for a little less than a minute before it vanished. One witness told the press that he was a plane spotter and amateur astronomer and had never seen anything like it before.

The Weird and Unexplainable

Perhaps Ireland's strangest mystery is the Jumping Church of Kildemock, located a couple of miles south of Ardee in County Louth. The church is a picturesque old ruin. Its history is unclear, but an archaeological excavation in 1953 uncovered a silver penny from the reign of Edward III who ruled from 1327-1377, so the building must be quite old. It is said to have already been a ruin in the 18th century when it made its claim to fame.

Why this church stands out is immediately apparent to any visitor. The western wall stands three feet off of its foundation. It hasn't fallen; it has simply moved. The foundation is clearly visible and it's quite obvious that the wall, which leans a bit precariously but remains upright, does not stand on any hidden foundation.

How could this happen? There are two stories to explain it, the first being that on Candlemas Day in 1715, a severe storm battered the ruined and abandoned church, blowing the wall off its foundation and settling it safely and intact nearly a meter from its original location. While this explanation stretches credulity, the other tale of how the wall moved is no more likely, unless one believes in miracles. The tale goes that a man who had been excommunicated was buried within the church grounds. The church was so disgusted by this sacrilege that it jumped back, leaving the sinner's grave outside of the church grounds.

The Jumping Church has some fierce competition as Ireland's strangest mystery. Another claimant is a spectacular vision in the sky that occurred on the clear, crisp morning of December 14, 1850. Around 6:30 in the morning, well before dawn, a family in the parish of Dunboe, County Derry saw the eastern horizon grow bright, as if the sun had planned to rise early, but the sun did not rise. Instead, two brightly glowing warships sailed into view in the sky. They stayed in sight for a few minutes before sailing away, only to be replaced by two phantom armies. As the December 31, 1850 edition of the *Northern Whig* reported, "[T]he eastern hemisphere became occupied by a grand panoramic representation of two armies approaching in warlike conflict…so distinctly visible was the representation, that their actual manoeuvres could be distinguished."

The startled family was spared a ghostly battle, because an officer from each army strode forward and fought a duel. The paper further reported that the entire display lasted an hour and a half before fading away to be replaced by the natural dawn.

Such visions were not unknown in the pre-modern era. The night before the Battle of Milvian Bridge in 312 CE, the Roman Emperor Constantine, then a Pagan, saw a vision of a cross in the sky with the words "Conquer by this sign" inscribed upon it. He ordered his soldiers to paint the sign on their shields, and they won the battle the next day, defeating Maxentius, Constantine's rival for the throne. Constantine became the undisputed emperor of the Roman Empire and later made Christianity its official religion. Other similar scenes, especially battles, have often been reported throughout time.

The sighting in Dunboe was not the first such vision in Ireland, nor was it the last. In October of 1796, the residents of the town of Youghal, County Cork saw a vision of a walled town hovering in the sky. The ghostly town reappeared on March 9, 1797, and again in June 1801. This third vision was the clearest, and witnesses described having seen mansions surrounded by bushes and white palings, with a forest growing behind them.

The September 8, 1860 edition of the *Coleraine Chronicle* reported on two such incidents. One which was said to have happened sometime in 1848 was reported by some fishermen on Loch Foyle. While fishing at night, they saw a massive parade of soldiers marching across the sky for some two hours. On September 2, 1860, a line of ships sailing from the eastern edge of the sky to the western appeared to a family in County Donegal. The ships were clearly seen "sailing down a river, whose high banks could be made out behind the ships." Other ships were moored by a fortress on a rock. During the 30 minutes the fleet remained visible, the vision was so clear that the family was able to see sailors as they worked on the deck.

On August 2, 1908, the people of Ballyconneely, Connemara saw a phantom city in the sky for three hours, with an assortment of houses clearly visible.

How might one explain these strange visions? The first reaction would be to dismiss them as a combination of Northern Lights and an overactive imagination. In each case, the sky was clear, so such a natural display would be visible. In the case of the fleet flying over County Donegal, the newspaper reported the vision had disappeared when the sky became cloudy. Note, however, that in each case, the scenes were witnessed by a group of people. Would everyone be able to identify the same objects in a display of the Northern Lights? Displays of the Northern Lights are not uncommon in Ireland, so it would have been quite familiar to people living in a time before electric lighting obscured their view of the night sky in a phenomenon disgruntled astronomers call "light pollution." Another explanation is that they had witnessed a strange fluke of optics that had somehow bent the light from a real scene somewhere else and thrown it as if projected onto the night sky, but how this might have happened is unclear. What does seem clear is that these nocturnal visions have become a thing of the past. No one sees phantom cities and armies in the skies anymore, which in some ways is quite a shame.

A more enduring and no less mysterious occurrence is the sighting of the "Lights of Crusheen," a pair of lights that look like flickering candles and are said to be a portent of doom.

These lights are seen on an island called Inchicronan, along a lake near the little village of Crusheen, County Clare. The island is uninhabited and has been so for many years. It's an interesting place, with a ruined medieval abbey and an old graveyard that has been the final resting place of the people of Crusheen for generations beyond counting. When the lights are seen on the island, the people of Crusheen believe one of their number will soon take up residence in the graveyard.

The lights have been seen ever since the Middle Ages, when, on a cold winter's night, a man from the village braved a storm to cross the causeway leading from the lakeshore to the island. The causeway could be slippery and dangerous in bad weather, and the fact that the man got across at all was a minor miracle. He had a good reason to risk himself; his mother was dying and he wanted to summon a monk to perform Last Rites. The monks were usually happy to help, but the only monk awake that night looked out the window at the foul weather and shook his head. "I'll go tomorrow when the weather has cleared," he said. "She'll keep until then."

Sadly, the woman died that night without the benefit of Last Rites. The monk lived many more years and remained unrepentant. Once he had died, however, God's punishment was swift. From then on, he was doomed to cross that lake to the village any time a spirit had to be taken up to heaven, a place he would never be allowed to enter.

Locals always know when the dead monk has to perform his duty, as two lights appear in the graveyard—one smaller and one larger—bobbing about six feet off the ground as if being carried by invisible people. They slowly cross the lake and enter the village to go to the house where the person is dying.

While this might seem like nothing more than a quaint local superstition, the phenomenon has been photographed numerous times and persists into the modern day. In 1967, physicist Dr. Wilfred Forbes studied the lights and interviewed eyewitnesses, but he was left baffled and unable to explain their origin.

Then there are Ireland's famous and mysterious weasel funerals. To be precise, the creatures called weasels in Ireland are actually Irish stoats (*Mustela erminea hibernica*). For some reason, the folks in rural areas call them weasels. A typical example of a weasel funeral was reported in the September 10, 1954 edition of *The Tyrone Constitution*: "A passing lorry killed a weasel near the residence of Mr. Hughie McGready, Mount Charles, Co Donegal. Messrs Gary Burke, Eugene Burke and Eamon Kelly were working nearby. They noticed the dead weasel on the road, but in ten minutes over fifty weasels had gathered to remove the remains. One weasel dragged the dead one away and was followed by some fifty 'mourners' each marching two abreast."

A picture of a stoat

The idea that weasels have funerals is widespread in Ireland, and it has been reported in Scotland as well. A request by the *Irish Times* for more information of this phenomenon from its readership brought in a flood of mail, some of it reporting on weasel funerals, and others warning that it was dangerous to be around the critters when they honored their dead because they might think the onlookers were the murderers. Actually killing a weasel could get people into some serious trouble, according to a letter sent in by a Mrs. Clark of Ballina, County Mayo: "Some men were cutting a meadow one day when they found some young stoats and killed them. Some time later, one of the men observed an old stoat come up and spit into a can of buttermilk the men had for drinking. The man at once threw away all the buttermilk. He said that had he not seen the stoat spitting into it, and had they drank the milk, they all would have been poisoned." Perhaps the stoat was angry at being called by its actual species.

Either way, it seems that visitors to Ireland should be sure to take weasels and fairies seriously, lest they find themselves in some serious trouble.

Online Resources

Other mysterious titles by Charles River Editors & Sean McLachlan

Other titles about Ireland on Amazon

Bibliography

Cassidy, Eddie. "Crowds still flock to 'moving statue' site at Ballinspittle, three decades on." *Irish Examiner*, July 22, 2015. http://www.irishexaminer.com/viewpoints/analysis/crowds-still-flock-to-moving-statue-site-at-ballinspittle-three-decades-on-343777.html Retrieved January 4, 2017.

Charles River Editors, and Sean McLachlan. *The Vikings in North America: The History and Legacy of the Norse Settlements in Greenland and Vinland.* 2015.

Fort, Charles. *The Complete Books of Charles Fort: The Book of the Damned / Lo! / Wild Talents / New Lands.* London: Dover Publications, Ltd, 1974.

McGowan, Joe. *Echoes of a Savage Land.* Cork: Mercier Press, 2001.

Michell, John. *The New View over Atlantis*. London: Thames & Hudson, 2001.

Moran, P.F., Archbishop. *The Voyage of St. Brendan the Abbot.* Privately published: Denis O'Donoghue, 1893.

Neil, Arnold. *Shadows in the Sky: The Haunted Airways of Britain.* Stroud, United Kingdom: The History Press, 2012.

Ó Súilleabháin, Seán. *Irish Folk Custom and Belief.* Cork: Mercier Press, 1977.

Pattison, Brynmor. "Holy stir as 'image of Virgin Mary' appears on house in Limerick." *Irish Mirror*, December 2, 2016. http://www.irishmirror.ie/news/irish-news/holy-stir-image-virgin-mary-9381161 Retrieved January 4, 2017.

Roche, Richard. *Tales of the Wexford Coast.* Enniscorthy: Duffry Press, 1993.

Severin, Tim. *The Brendan Voyage: Sailing to America in a Leather Boat to Prove the Legend of the Irish Sailor Saints.* New York City: Modern Library, 2000.

The Telegraph. "Virgin Mary spotted in Irish Tree". July 9, 2009. http://www.telegraph.co.uk/news/newstopics/howaboutthat/5790527/Virgin-Mary-spotted-in-Irish-tree.html Retrieved January 4, 2017.

Wilde, Lady. *Irish Cures, Mystic Charms & Superstitions.* New York City: Sterling Publishing Company, Inc., 1991.

Free Books by Charles River Editors

We have brand new titles available for free most days of the week. To see which of our titles are currently free, click on this link.

Discounted Books by Charles River Editors

We have titles at a discount price of just 99 cents everyday. To see which of our titles are currently 99 cents, click on this link.

Made in the USA
San Bernardino, CA
07 August 2017